All My Unspoken Thoughts

Deborah Tyack

BookLeaf Publishing

All My Unspoken Thoughts © 2022
Deborah Tyack

All rights reserved.

No part of this publication may be reproduced, stored in a retrieval system, or transmitted, in any form or by any means, electronic, mechanical, photocopying, recording or otherwise, without the prior written permission of the presenters.

Deborah Tyack asserts the moral right to be identified as author of this work.

Presentation by *BookLeaf Publishing*

Web: www.bookleafpub.com

E-mail: info@bookleafpub.com

ISBN: 978-93-95755-55-9

First edition 2022

*To my family, for their unwavering support
in all of my endeavours.*

ACKNOWLEDGEMENT

Thank you to my sister for her letter 'O'.

Always in my Heart

Memories of a forgotten past,
Like files stored away too fast,
Misplaced in our busy minds,
But kept always in our hearts.

Short term and long term,
Memories to confirm,
What happened here?
It's all unclear.

Replaced by the stories told,
To fill the gaps, we start to mould,
Our minds forget and change around,
But our hearts remember beyond bounds.

Lonely Fields

I walk around aimlessly, awkwardly,
Never really knowing,
Never really going anywhere.
All alone in the busy streets,
Knowing I don't belong there.
I may see fields of flowers,
And the grass may be green.
But it just seems so dull to me.
And the days may go by,
As the sunflowers die.
And sometimes I just want to be myself.
Is that alright?

Life of a Flower

From the seed of a fruit, they come forth,
With no expectations of being taught.
They don't know how to grow on their own,
So, we water and feed them with mineral soil.
The life of a flower though may be short,
Sprouts colours of sorrow and joy.
With reds, yellows and blues,
Fields get covered and so do your shoes.
By themselves or in a group,
Their colours still shine on through.
Have a look at them today,
For tomorrow they may wither away.

My Island

I come from an island that is mostly unknown,
And on the maps its barely shown.
It's just a dot in the big wide ocean,
And people there are always in motion.

With waters as clear as crystals,
And sand as white as snow,
My island though small and unknown,
Harbours too many people and has outgrown.

You and I

Like two peas in a pod, we were with each other.
We came into this world, yellow and purple
were our colours. Oh, so different, that we were,
a bond so strong it was unheard. Fights with
bites and bruises up our arms, we learnt to play,
rather rough, but it was fun. You and I will take
on this world, as a singer and police girl. I love
you with no bounds and would take a bullet for
you anytime. But to those that were there before
and the one that came just after, I love you all
too, but you and I are like glue, and we should
maybe be locked up in a zoo.

Underwater

The water never flows the way I want it to.
It decides for itself just like my thoughts do.
And I would try to place obstacles on its way,
But underwater they sink or float astray.

My thoughts swim free in this underwater sea,
Hoping to be heard without a word.
But that won't do, in this deep blue,
For here comes trouble, as I speak only bubbles.

Never Give Up

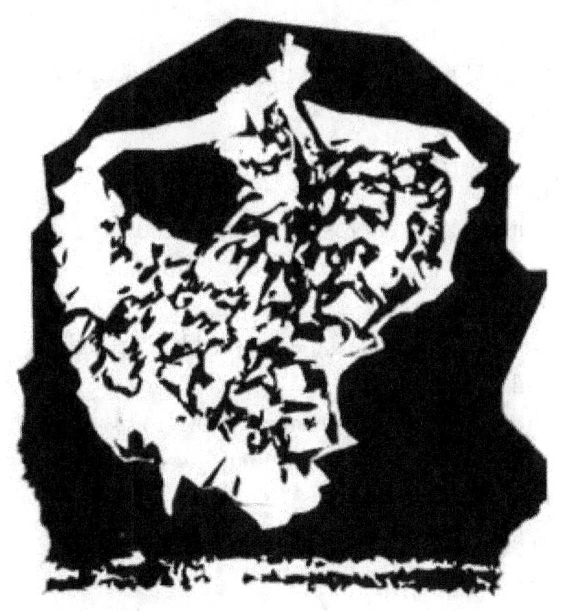

You have to stand on your own 2 feet,
So, don't let people steal your beat.
Cause this life could be bittersweet,
As the puzzle is incomplete.

But stand up tall, and listen to the call.
Dance as though you'd never fall,
And if you have to, then crawl,
But make your way up that wall.

Superhero

I would have a double life and be a superhero at
night.
I would patrol the streets with my mask and
fight.
With my powers I will protect this town.
Even if it means that I could go down.

But I don't have a superpower like I thought I
had.
I'm pretty average from my looks to my stats.
I thought I new my mind, but I was quite off
track.
What was I thinking living my life on the line
like that.

But to be a hero is not all that.
I don't need a mask or cape or patrol the night.
What I need is courage to stand up for what is
right.
I may not be a superhero but I'm a hero alright.

Palm of your Hand

You've been there through it all,
You've seen my highs and my lows,
Giving me a hand as I grow.

Not once have you looked down,
Avoiding my gaze, or avoiding my eyes,
All thanks to you I can now stand proud.

You've held my hand, you've held my heart.
You've held my soul, you've held my life,
All in the palm of your hand.

You've made me who I am today,
Even through the hardest of days,
I hope my love for you is conveyed.

One Life

It may take a year,
Or maybe my whole life.
It may take a month,
Or maybe some more time.

Many years have passed,
And I'm older now.
I'll live as I can before I die,
As I only have one life.

Kept in your Prayers

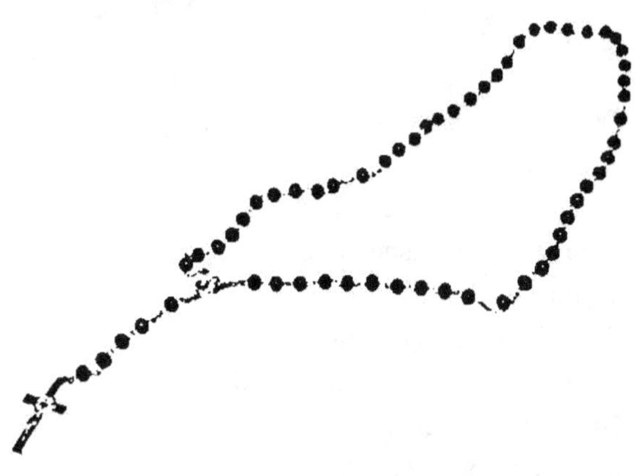

Even as the snow falls and turns into an
avalanche,
Even as the rain falls and forms a raging flood.
Your prayers have blessed so many from far and
wide,
I wish that you've prayed for me in this life.
It may seem selfish or out of place,
But sometimes I need a guiding grace.
Your prayers have guided those lost in storms,
I'm lost and don't know which way is north.
A prayer can be all it takes,
To make the sick better or help them find their
way.
So please I ask of you,
Keep me in your prayers today.

Everyone

When the weather is turning bad,
And the storm is approaching,
The rain is pouring.
Everyone has wished once,
To turn back the clock of time.
For things happened then,
That we wish we could rewind.
But what happened then,
Made us who we are today.
And I know for a fact,
That most people are better,
Because of those days.

New Beginning

I'm asking for forgiveness,
For everything that has been said and done.
I'm asking for forgiveness,
For every time I let you down.

I wish I could understand what was on your
mind,
So that I could help you and be some sort of
guide.
I wish that I'd stop arguing every time that we
talked,
So that I could hold a conversation without
making it short.

I'm asking for forgiveness,
For letting my anger control me.
I'm asking for forgiveness,
For this new beginning.

Treasured Lesson

The moment you walked into my life,
And talked like you were mine,
I saw it in your eyes.

The moment you said I love you,
It was too soon to be true.
I saw straight through your lies.

I won't be played like those before,
So, I'll tell the world what I saw unfold.
With this song that is played on repeat in my
head,
I'll tell the world of what's been said.

So, thank you for this beat and melody
That I can hear constantly.
I won't forget this passing thought
And treasure this lesson taught.

Holiday

We have travelled overseas and through the sky,
All for the one purpose, to see your blinding
smiles.
Remembering that no one can beat your fruit
cake,
We bear gifts for all in an overloaded suitcase.

But by the time we must say our goodbyes,
Our tears keep flowing from our eyes.
Wishing we could stay for a longer time,
And enjoy the sun with freshly press limes.

We say thank you for this holiday,
Spent with family every day.
We've made memories to last a year,
As we take home some souvenirs.

One Mistake

Can you really give someone a second chance?
Can you ever truly treat them the same?
Can you believe that they wouldn't do it again?
Cause all it takes is one mistake.

Just like water rushing through the mountains,
But getting stopped and forming a lake.
It's a wonder we like to share,
But a mistake we must repair.

Underneath the Sand Below

Walking on the beach,
Sand crumbling at your feet,
What could there be,
Buried underneath?

A treasure from years ago,
Or a shipwreck buried below,
A sanctuary for tomorrow,
A place some may call home.

With tunnels dug out by hand,
And pillars of solid sand,
Scattered throughout the land
Are mysteries to understand.

An adventure for those who dare,
With mystery in the air,
But please do not despair
For will you take all or share?

Good Nights

As the rain falls, I remember the nights we would stay up talking for hours and end up laughing too loud. At times over something funny, but mostly because someone breathed strangely.
We were the only ones ever awake at these times, making it harder to stop when one of us would start. But with the continuous phrase of good night, another round of laughs broke out; and this continued as the rain fell and the moon bid us farewell.

Hopes and Dreams

Maybe life is just a game,
Made for us to surly break.
Hopes and dreams seem like nothing,
But are rays of light in this ending.

The eyes of children though small, they seem,
To harbour all of humanities hopes and dreams.
The adults of this world have chosen to shut
their eyes,
While the little ones stare in wonder and delight.

Troubled Child

I was always a troubled child,
I never thought that I'd see the light.
I always had dreams within me,
I just never saw them coming free.

The dreams within me were,
Trying hard to break out.
Making my job hard,
Hiding from the world outside.

The dreams deep down inside,
Are now breaking down all my walls.
To see the world outside,
I might just let them out.

I can now see my light burning bright,
It has taken years but that's fine.
It may have been years but I'm still myself,
As I'm still that troubled child.

Smile your Clouds Away

I know you're gorgeous on the inside and out.
I know you struggle with the challenges of life.
But I know that you're strong, and you prove it
every day.
With your smile, and your laugh and the jokes
that you make.

I know that you're smart, and I know that you're
brave.
I know that you'll make it through today.
So, crack a smile and laugh away,
Keep those jokes coming for the future can wait.

With a change of mind, and a change of heart.
The world becomes bright and blinds your sight.
So, say goodbye to your clouds, and to the rain
good night.
It's a new day and it's your time to shine.

www.ingramcontent.com/pod-product-compliance
Lightning Source LLC
LaVergne TN
LVHW021346200726
843509LV00014B/2699